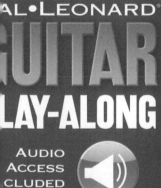

HAL•LEONARD®
GUITAR PLAY-ALONG

AUDIO ACCESS CLUDED

PLAYBACK+
·d • Pitch • Balance • Loop

SMOOTH JAZZ

VOL. 124

T0066484

CONTENTS

To access audio visit:
www.halleonard.com/mylibrary

8263-0176-6050-7882

ISBN 978-1-4950-7896-5

HAL•LEONARD®

Visit Hal Leonard Online at
www.halleonard.com

Contact us:
Hal Leonard
7777 West Bluemound Road
Milwaukee, WI 53213
Email: info@halleonard.com

In Europe, contact:
Hal Leonard Europe Limited
42 Wigmore Street
Marylebone, London, W1U 2RN
Email: info@halleonardeurope.com

In Australia, contact:
Hal Leonard Australia Pty. Ltd.
4 Lentara Court
Cheltenham, Victoria, 3192 Australia
Email: info@halleonard.com.au

After Hours (The Antidote)

By Ronald Les Albert Simpson

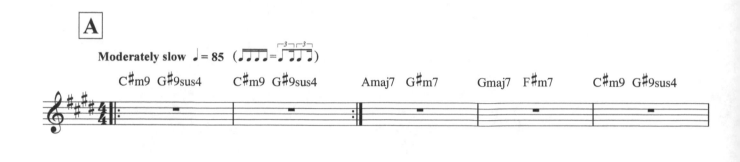

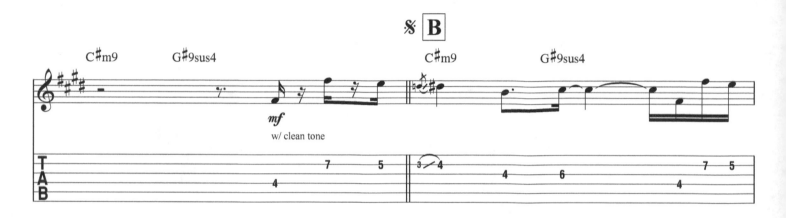

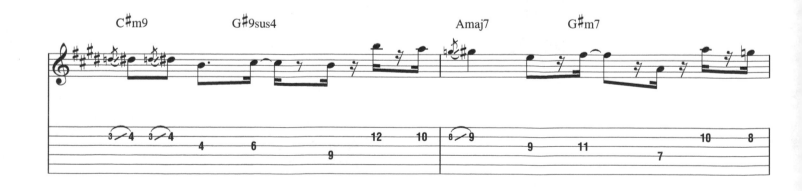

3rd time, substitute Fill 1

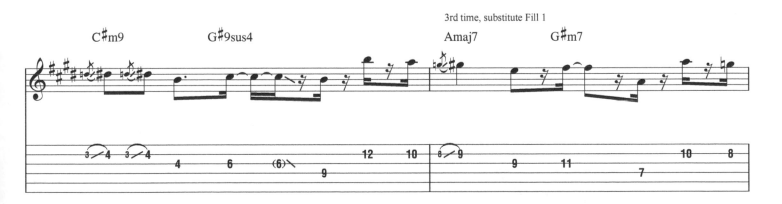

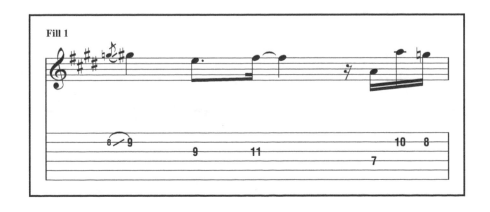

C

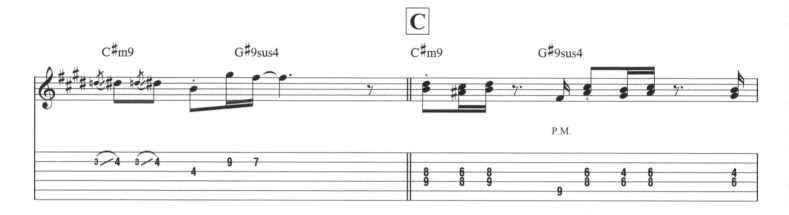

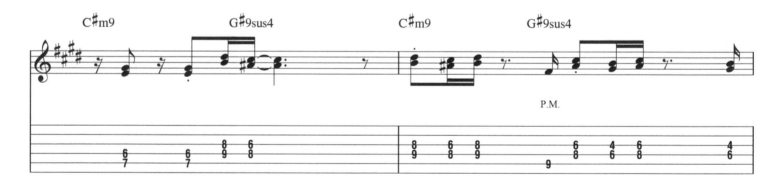

To Coda 2

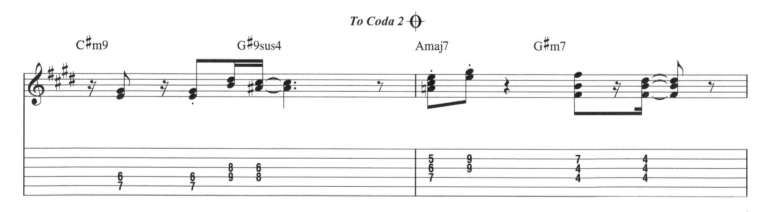

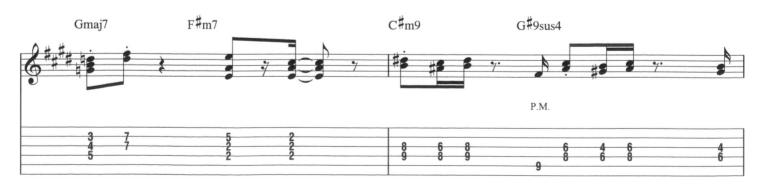

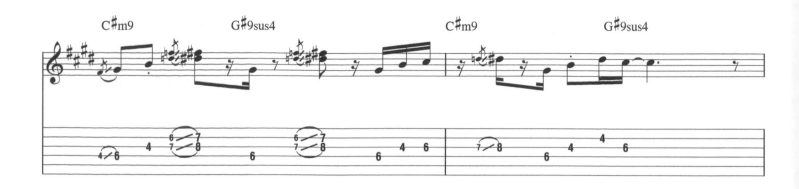

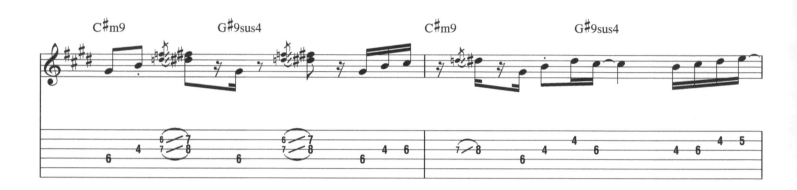

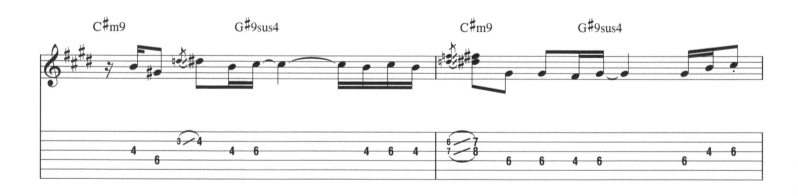

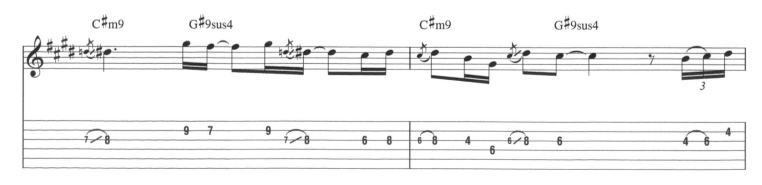

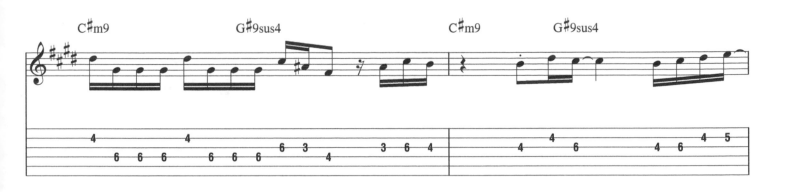

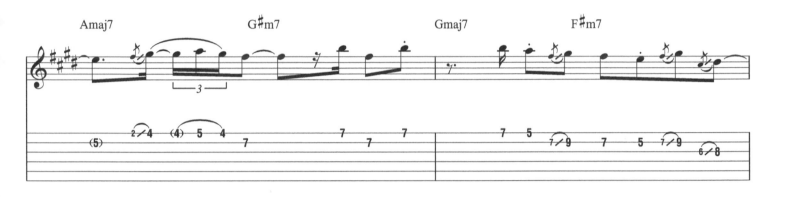

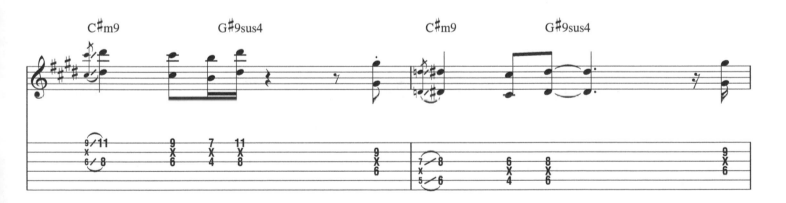

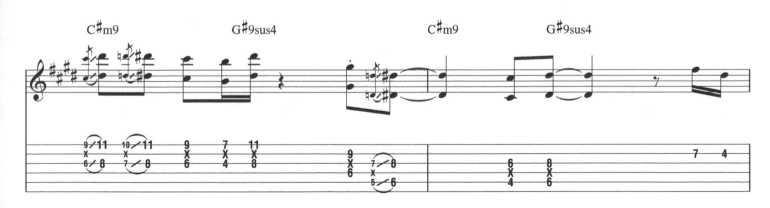

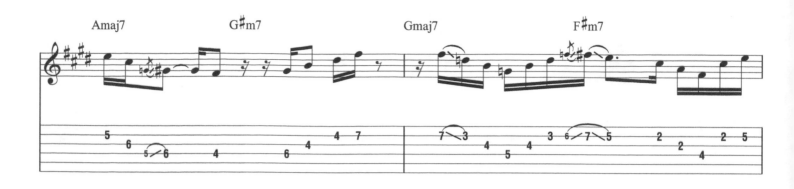

D.S.S. al Coda 2

E

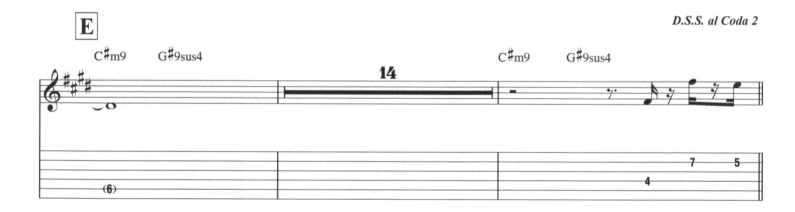

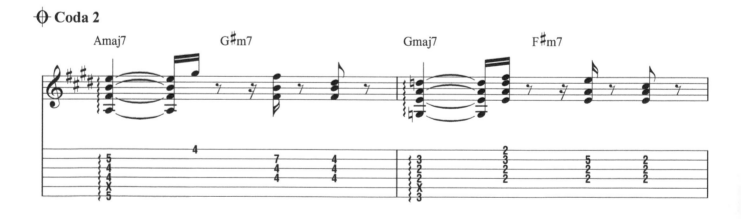

Breezin'

Words and Music by Bobby Womack

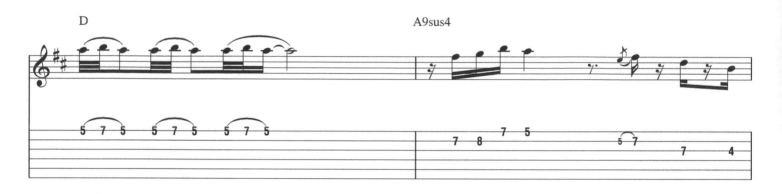

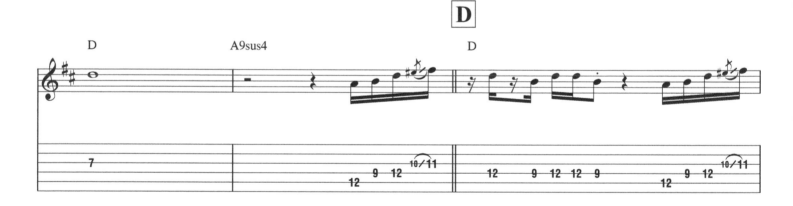

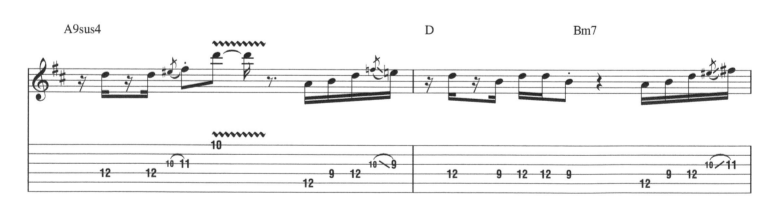

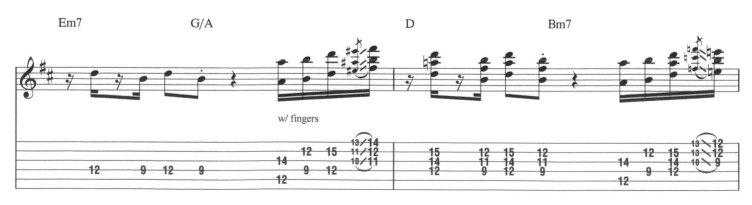

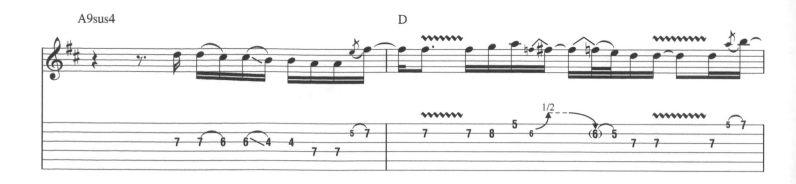

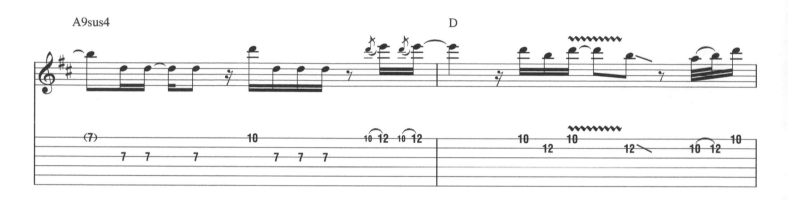

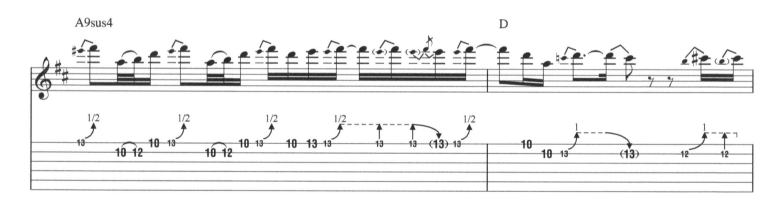

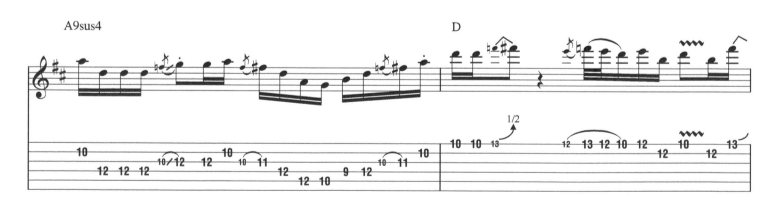

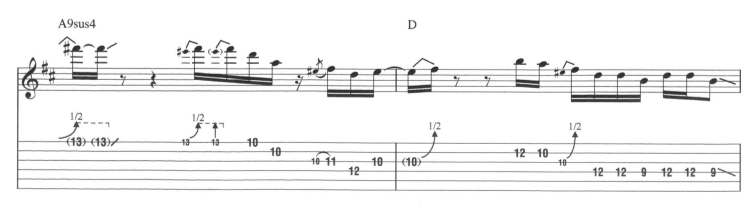

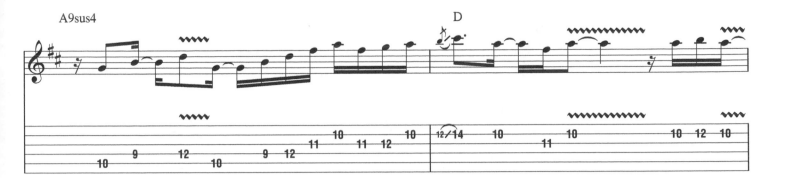

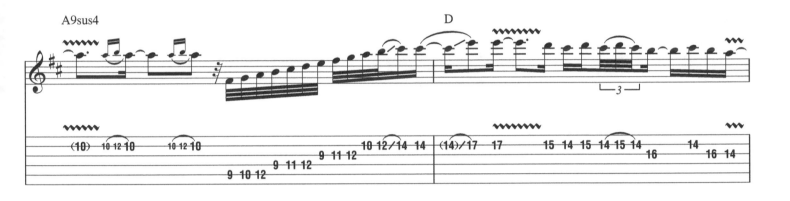

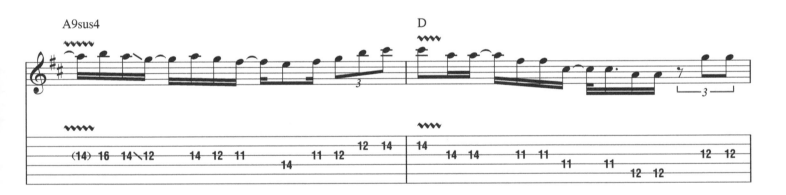

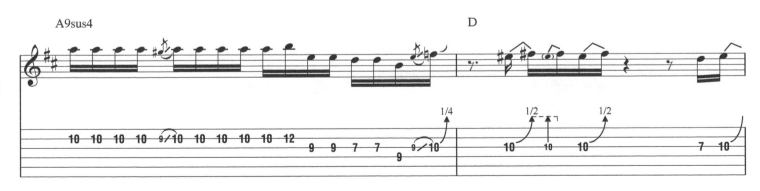

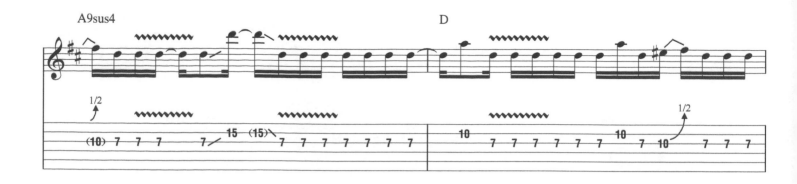

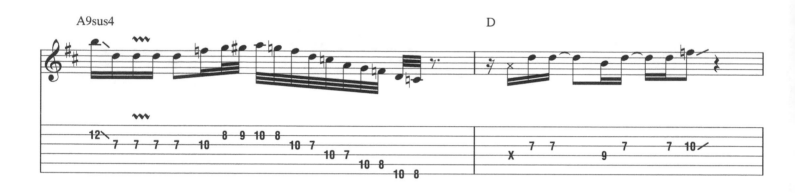

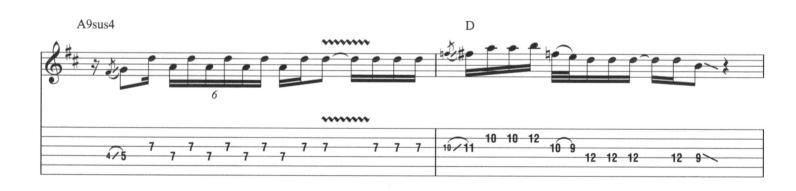

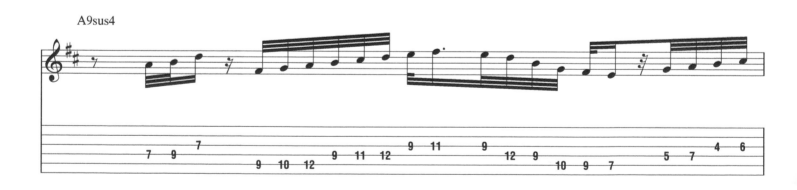

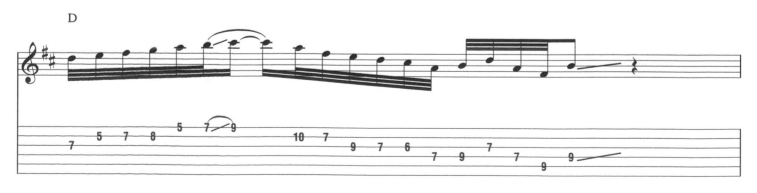

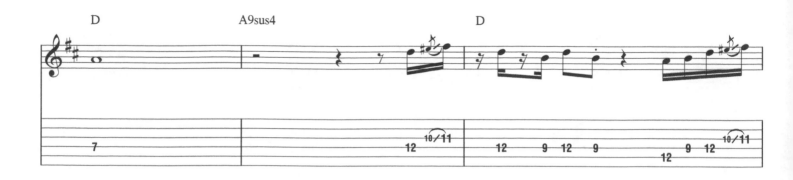

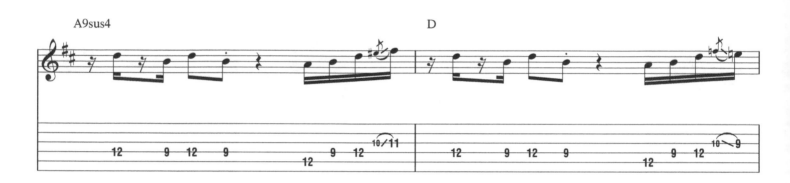

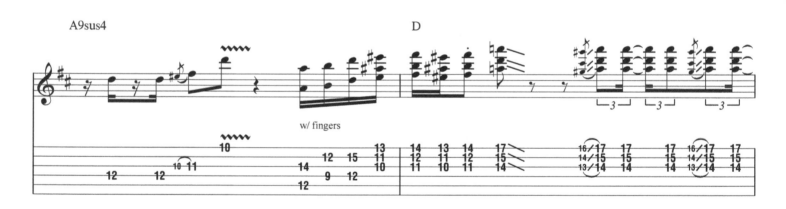

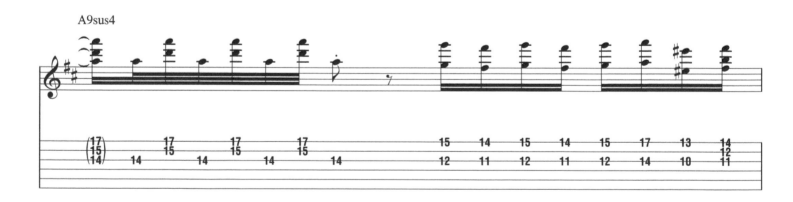

Cause We've Ended as Lovers

Words and Music by Stevie Wonder

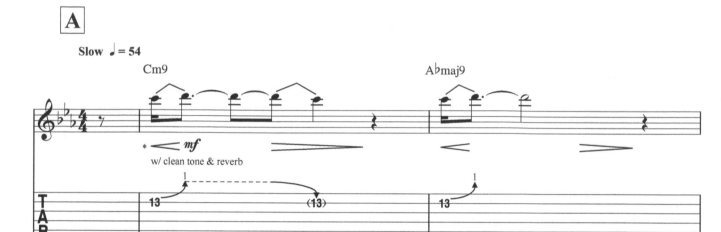

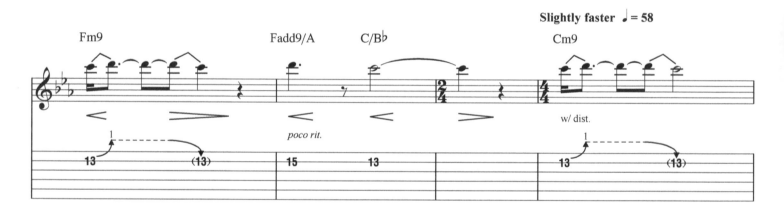

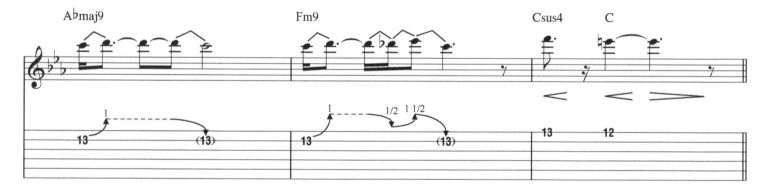

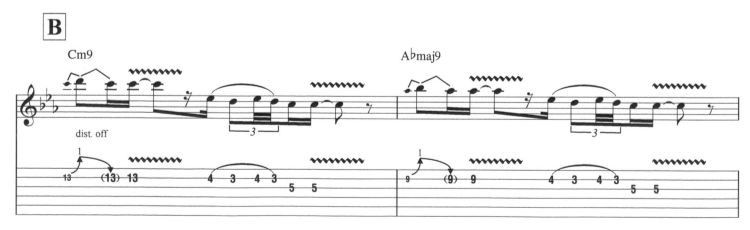

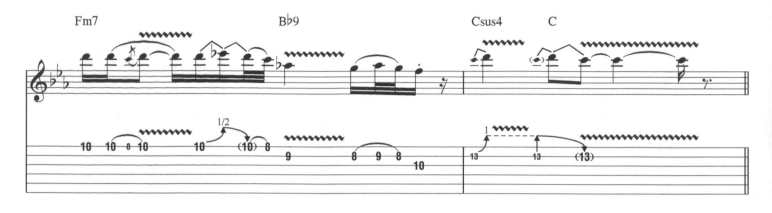

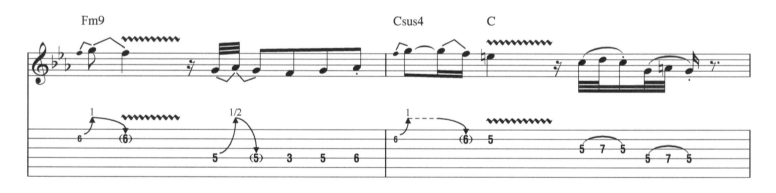

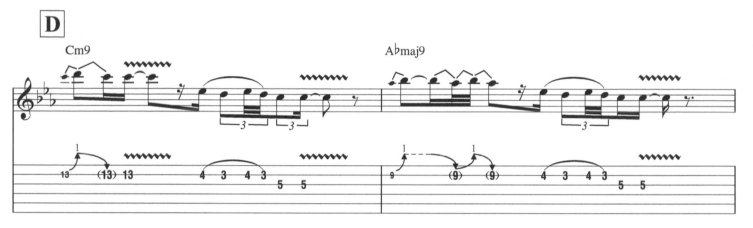

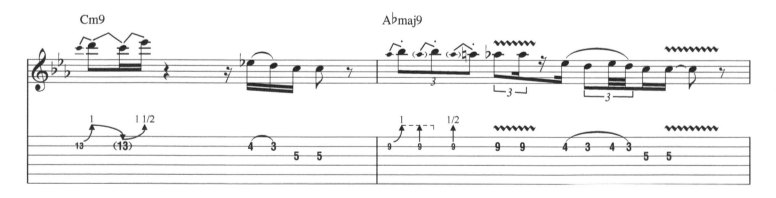

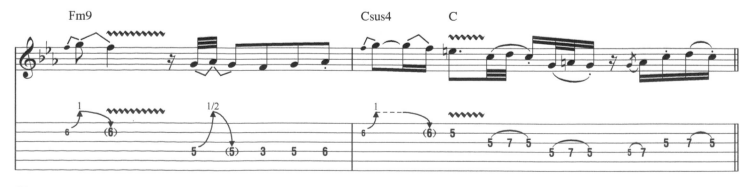

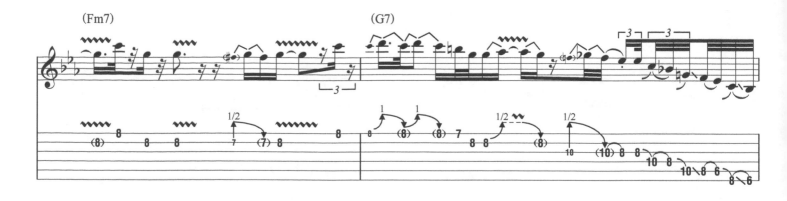

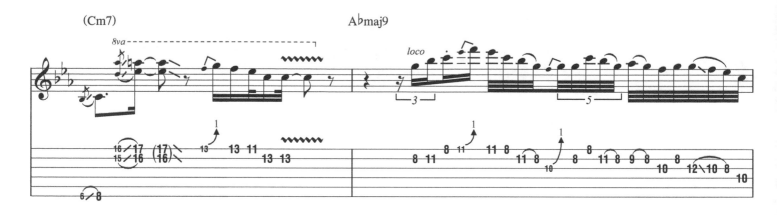

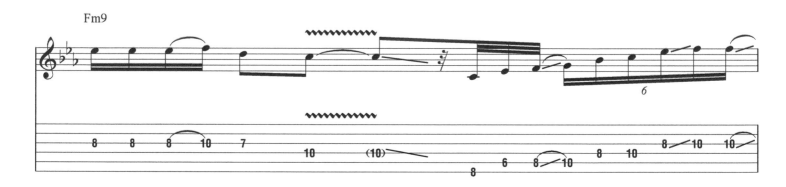

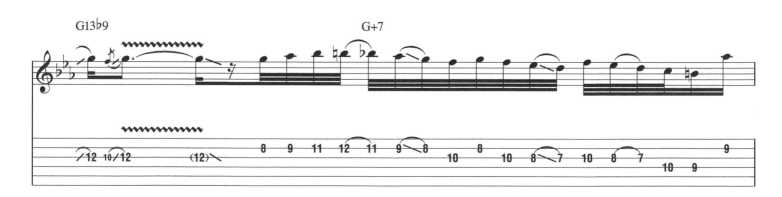

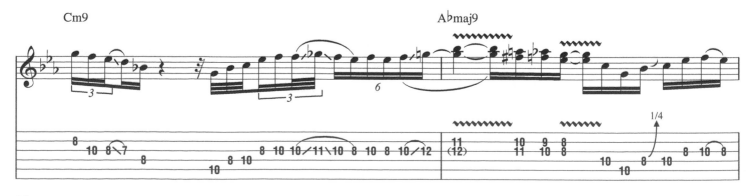

High Five

By Chuck Loeb

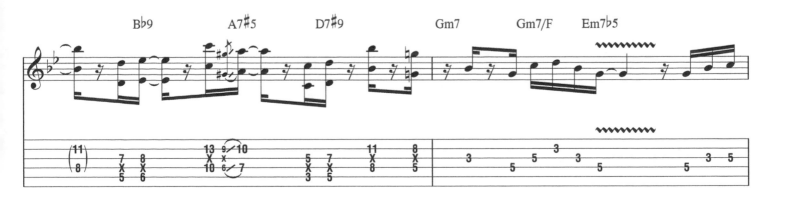

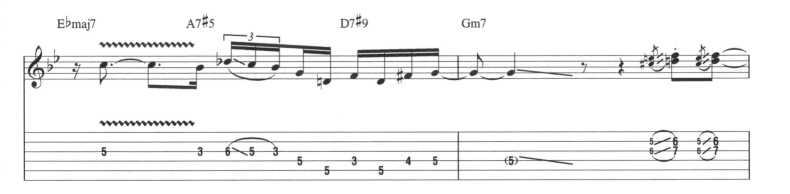

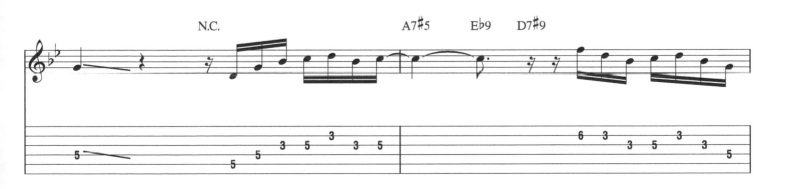

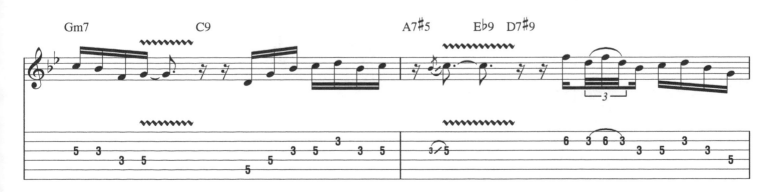

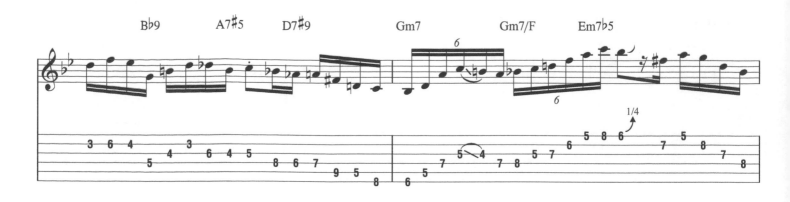

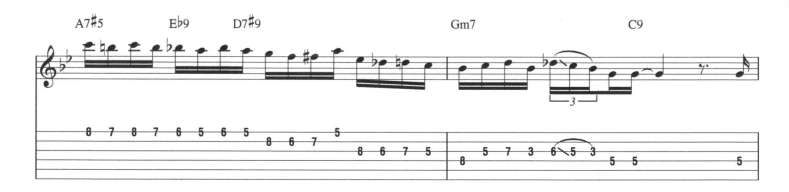

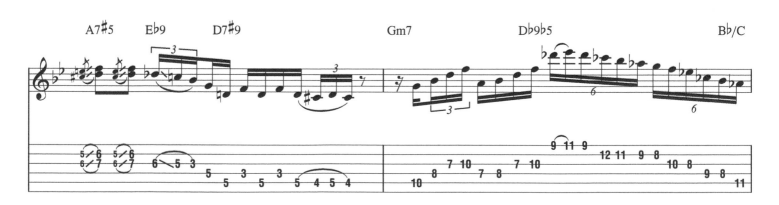

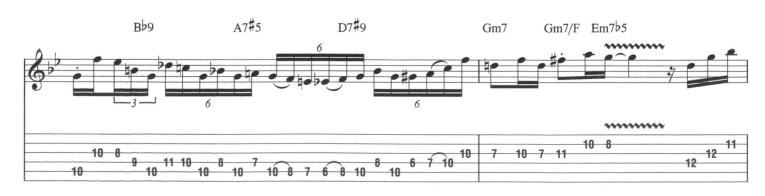

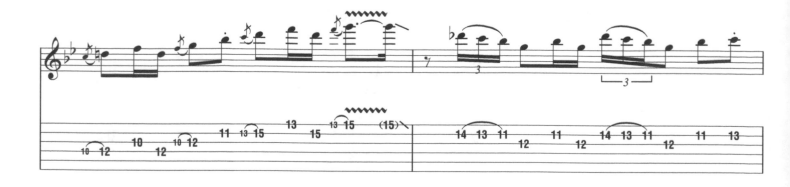

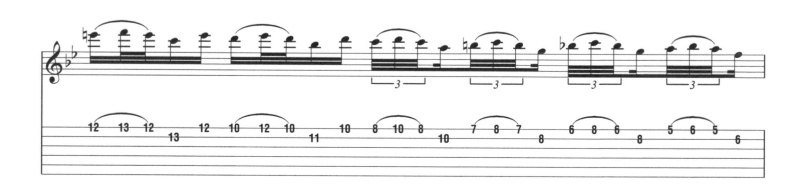

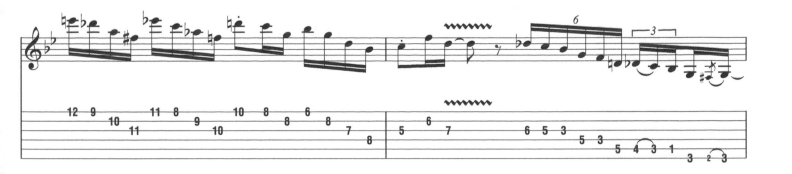

Begin fade

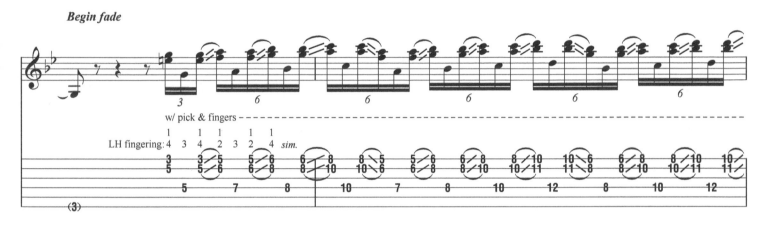

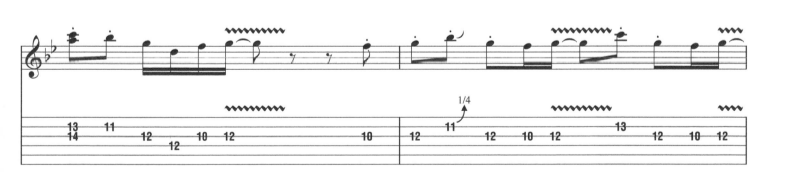

Fade out

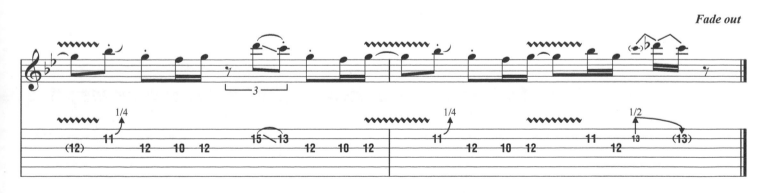

Night Rhythms

By Lee Ritenour

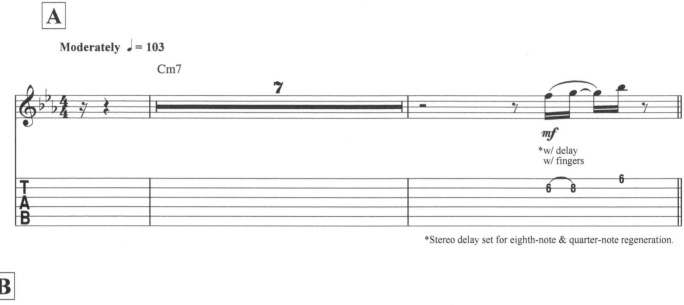

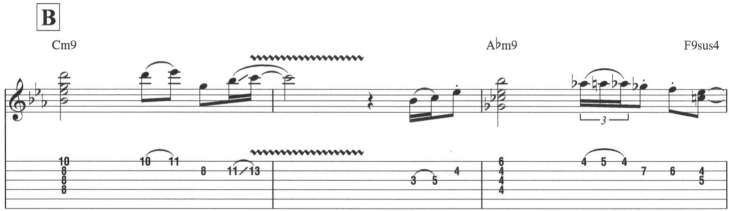

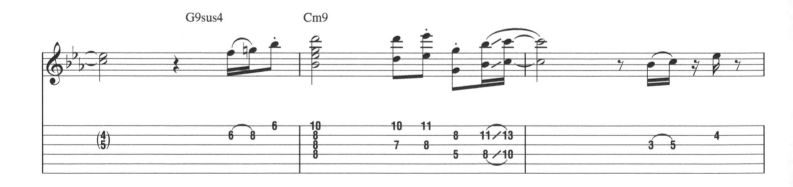

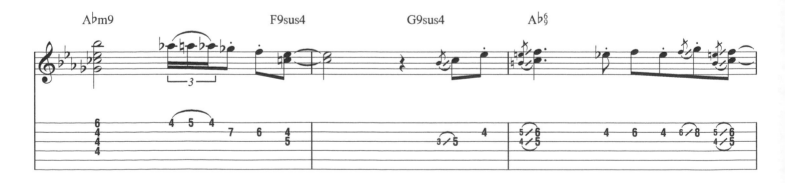

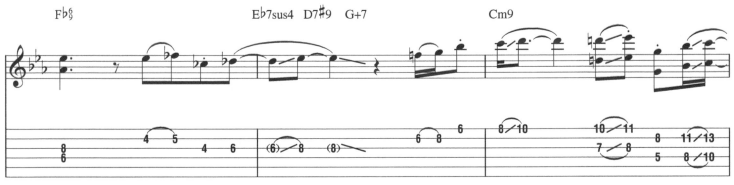

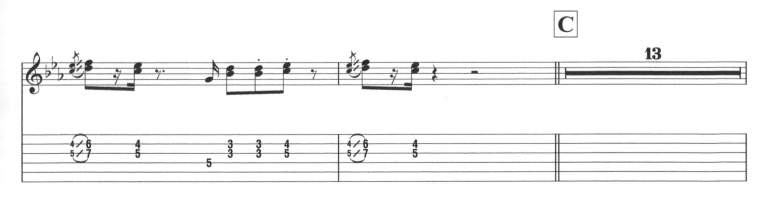

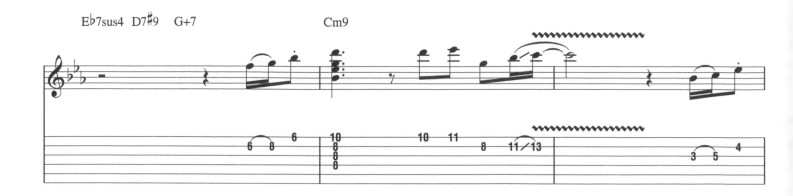

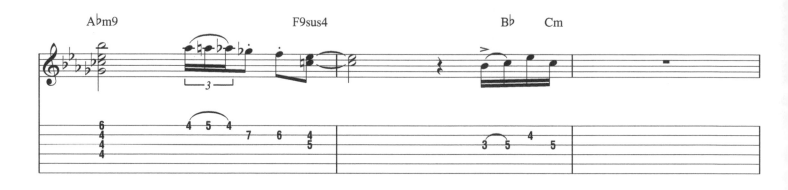

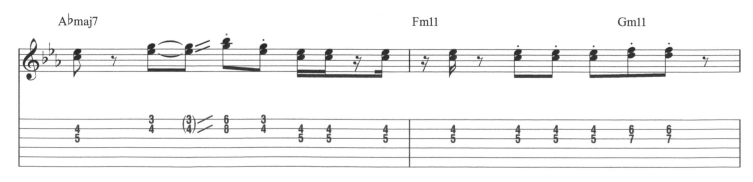

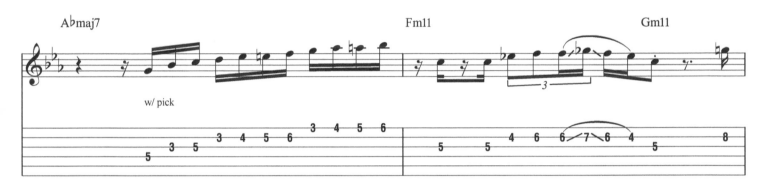

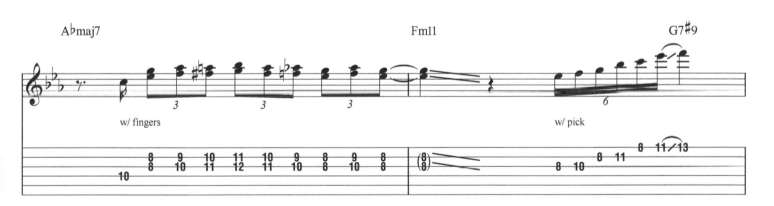

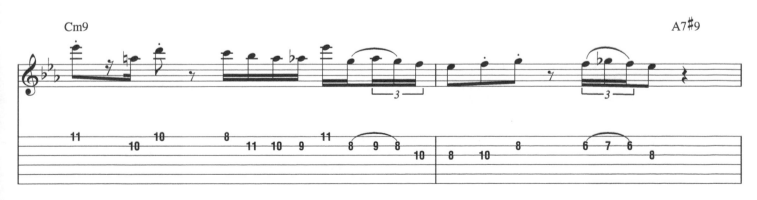

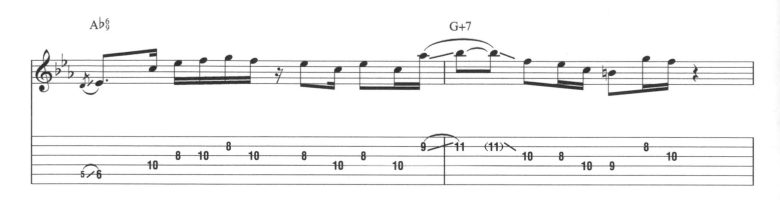

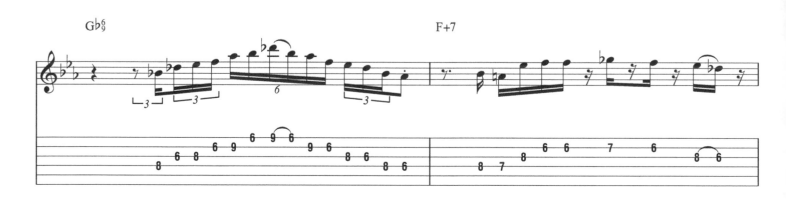

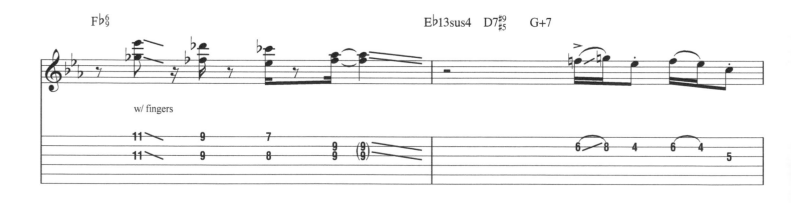

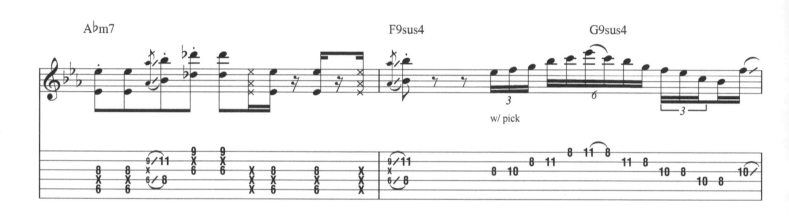

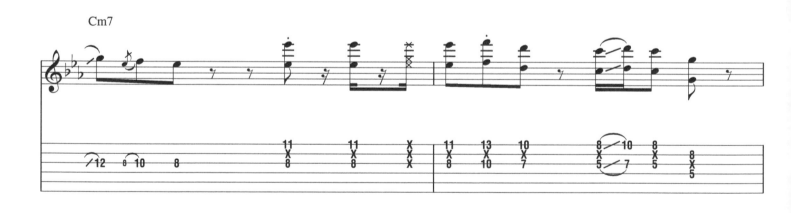

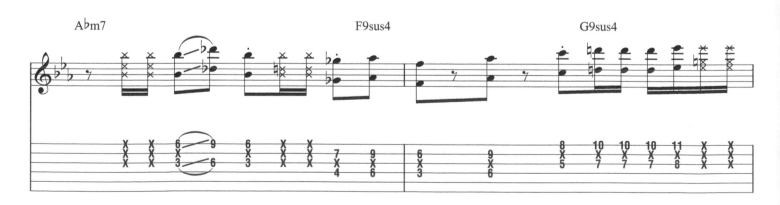

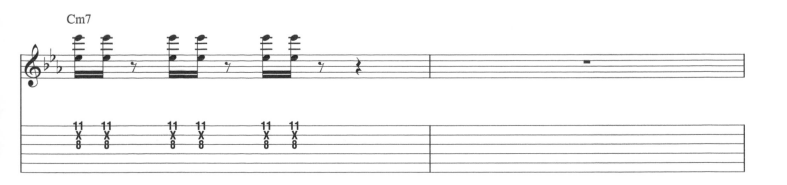

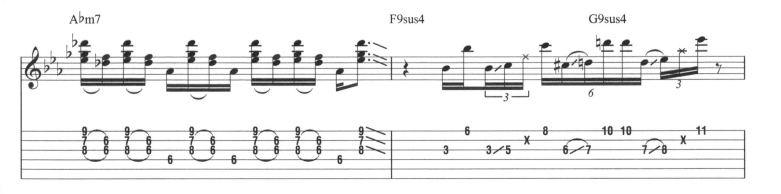

Begin fade

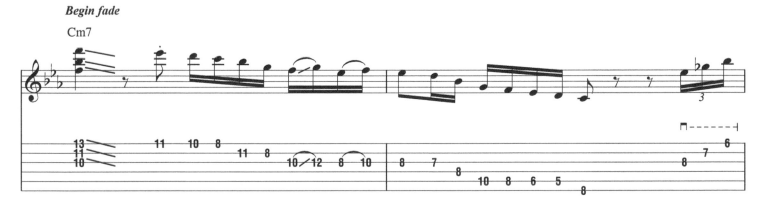

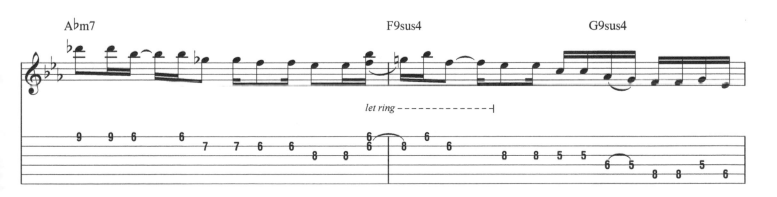

Fade out

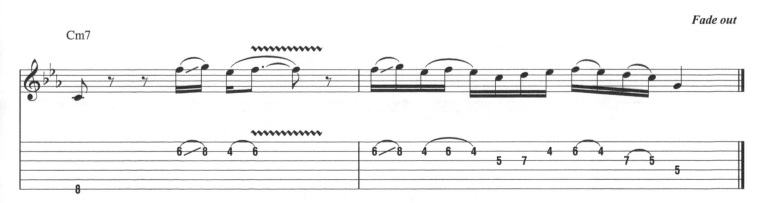

Smiles and Smiles to Go

By Larry Carlton

*Play doublestops w/ upstroke throughout, emphasizing higher note. (Unless otherwise indicated.)

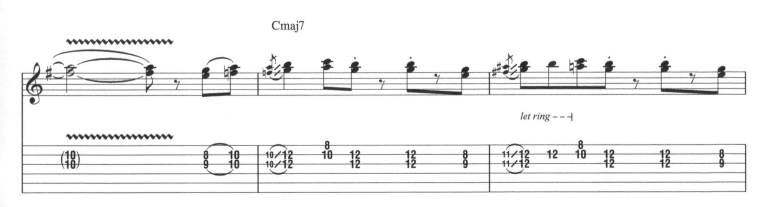

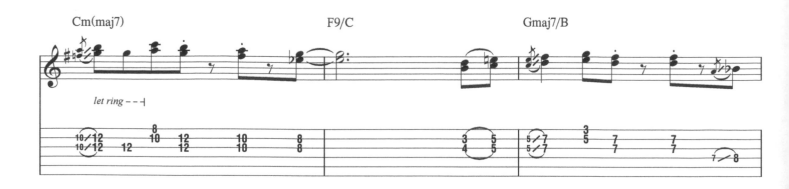

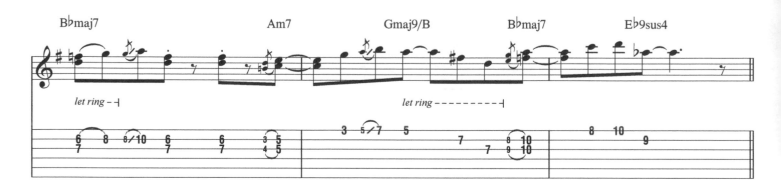

C

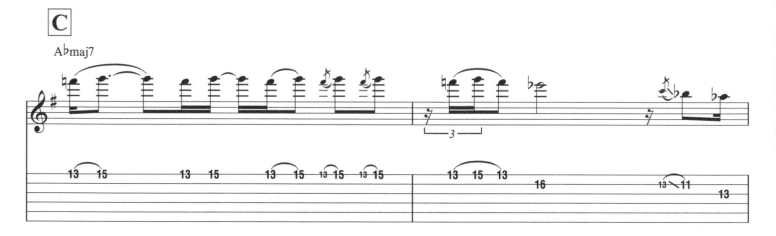

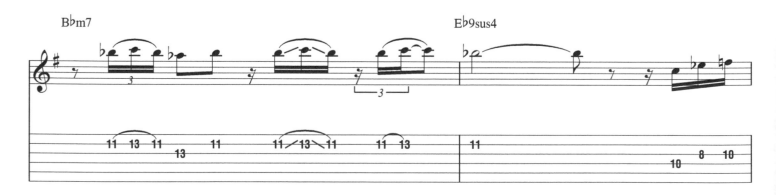

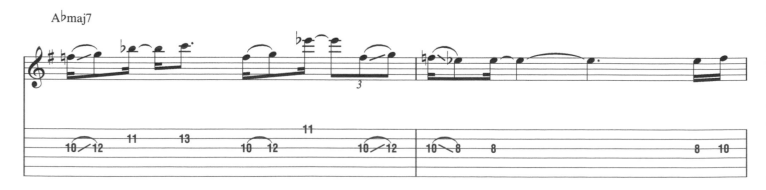

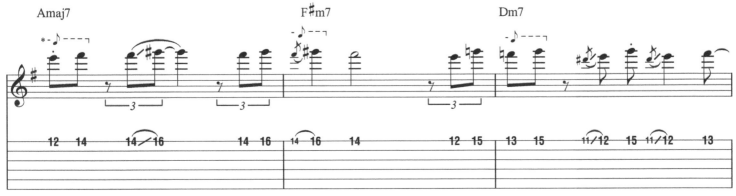

*Played behind the beat.

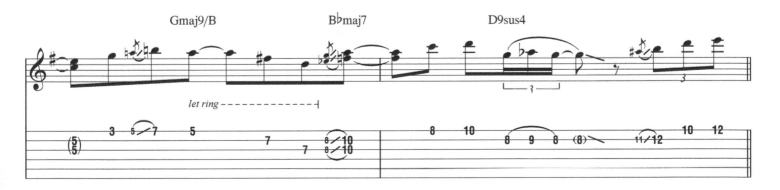

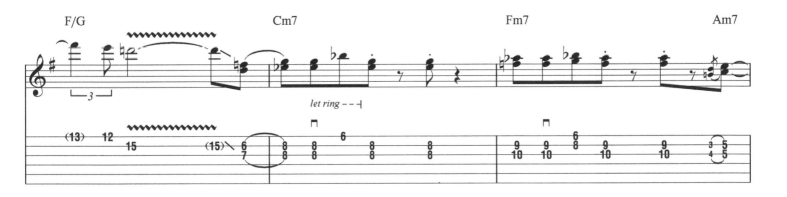

D

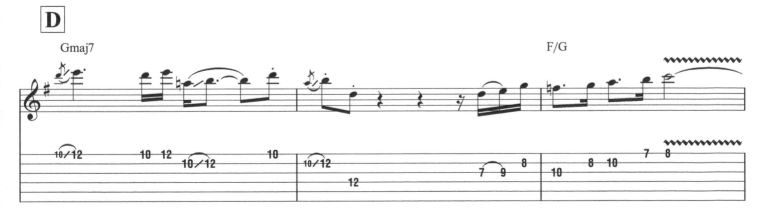

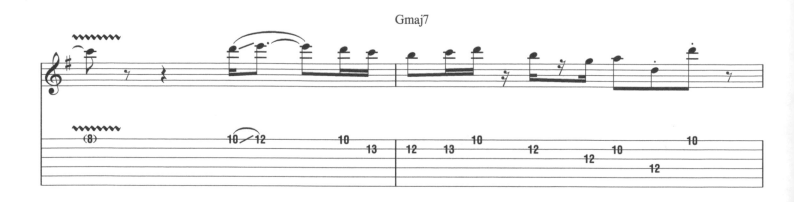

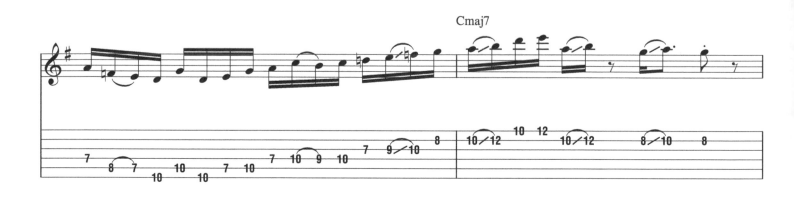

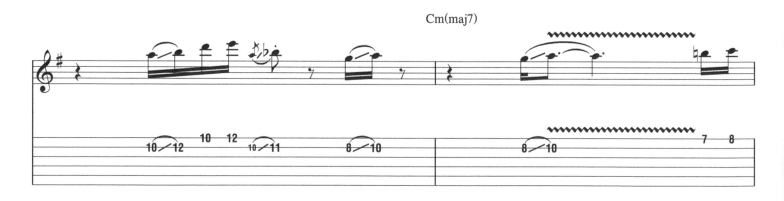

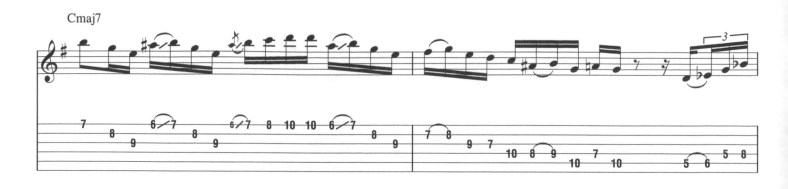

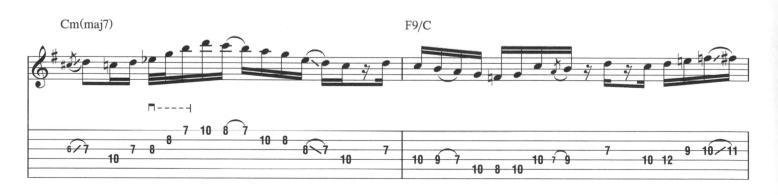

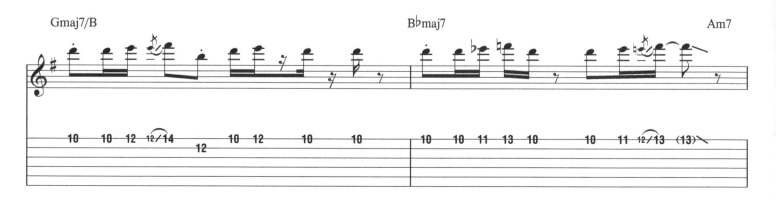

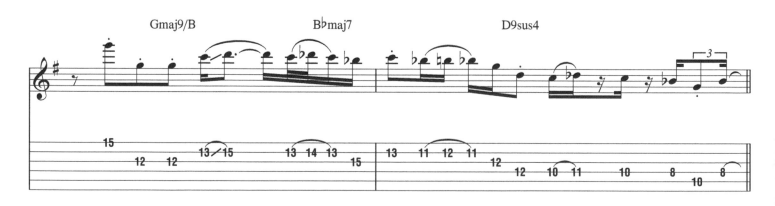

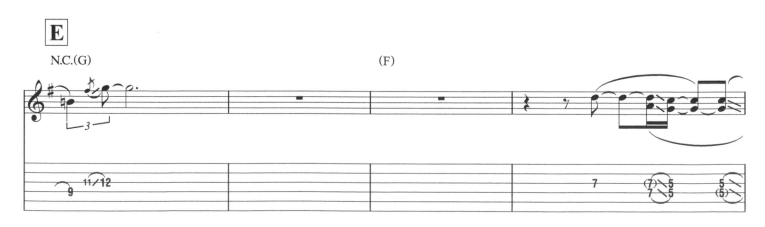

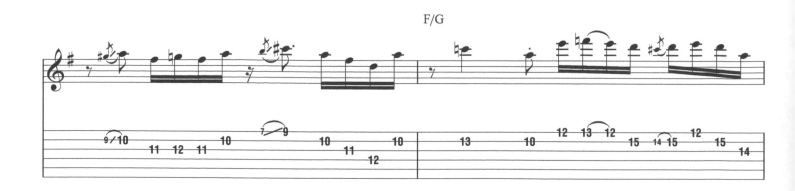

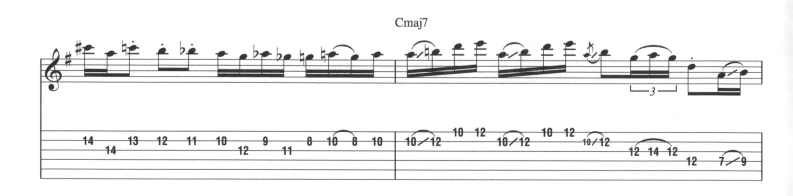

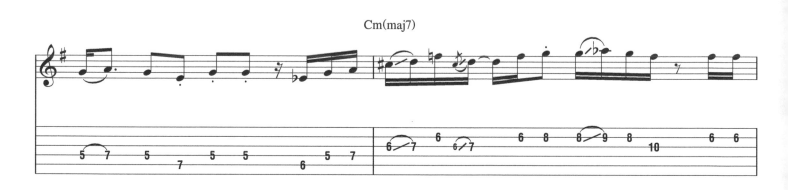

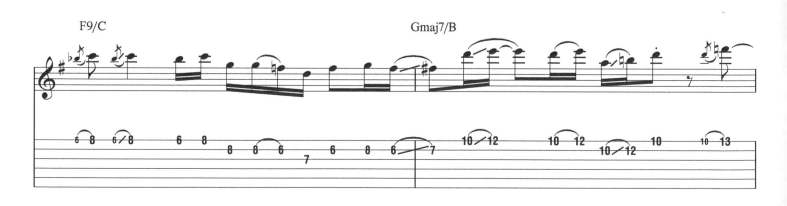

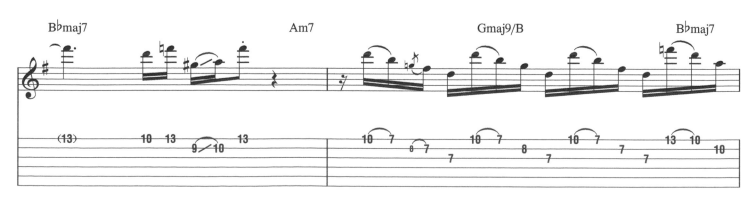

Up 'n' at 'Em

By Christopher Allen Bolden, Norman C. Brown, Paul Raymond Brown and Wirlie Lee Morris

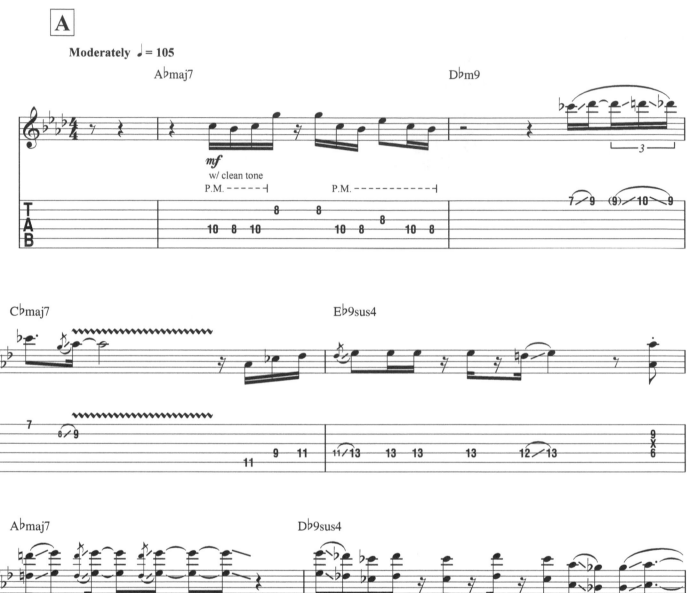

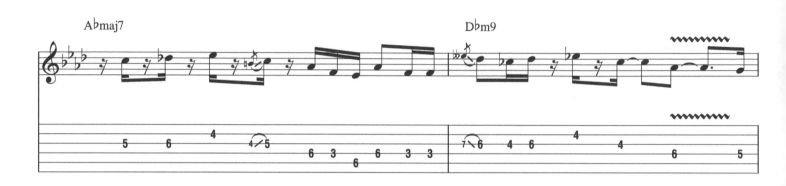

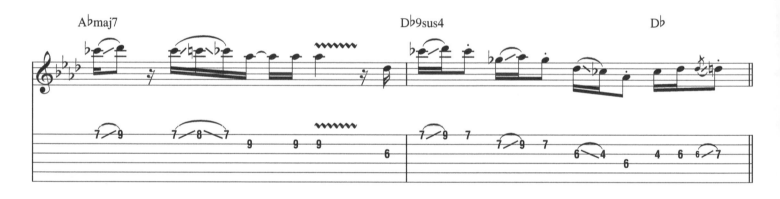

D

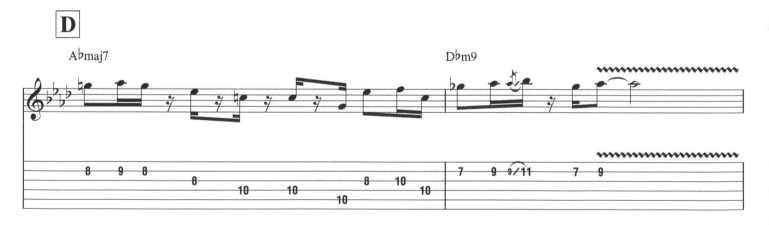

F

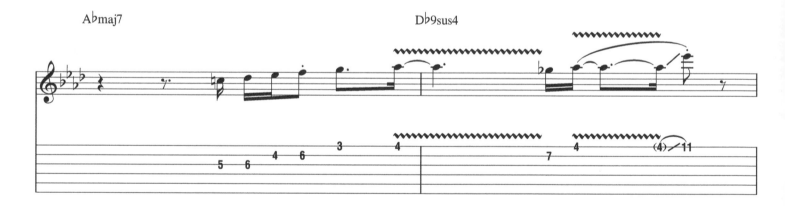

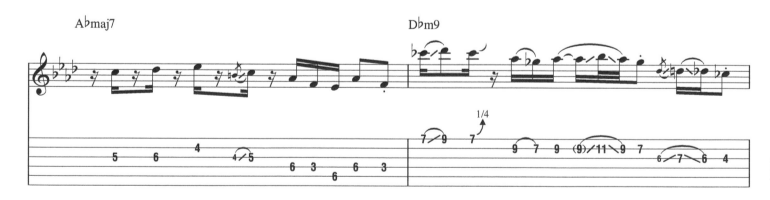

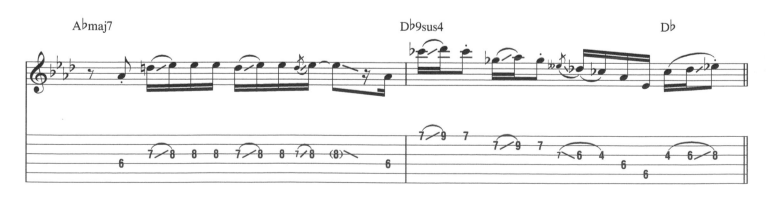

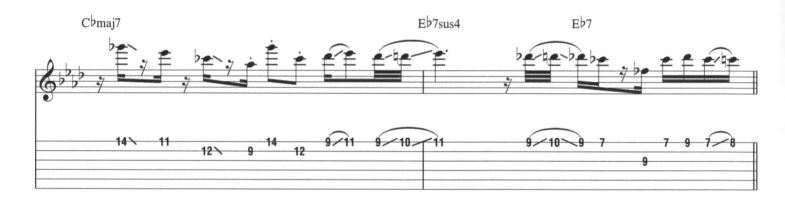

I

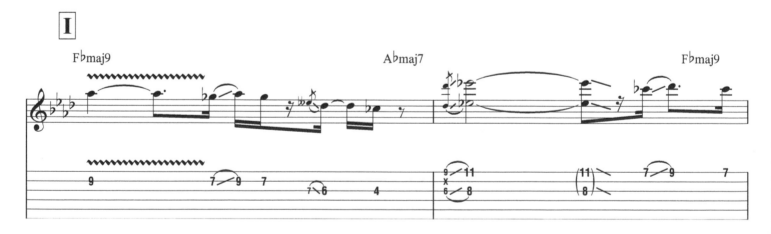

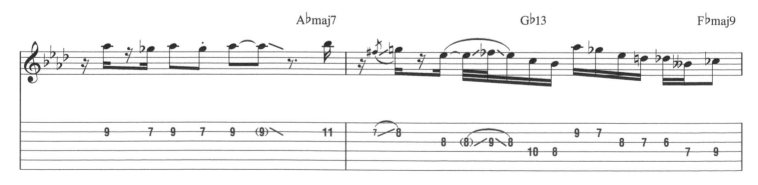

Wishful Thinking

Words and Music by Earl Klugh

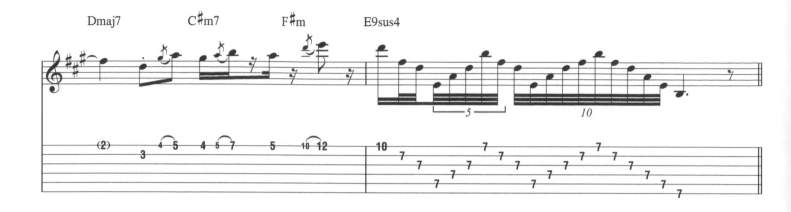

D

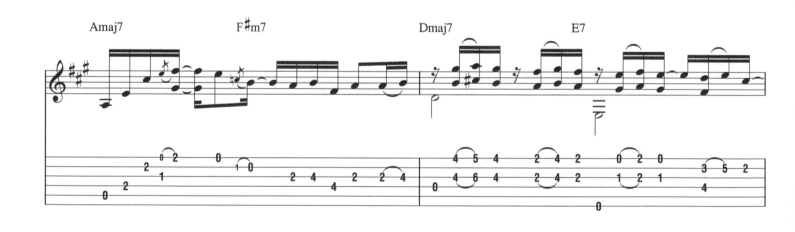

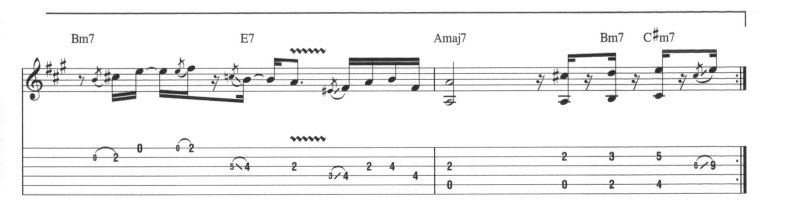

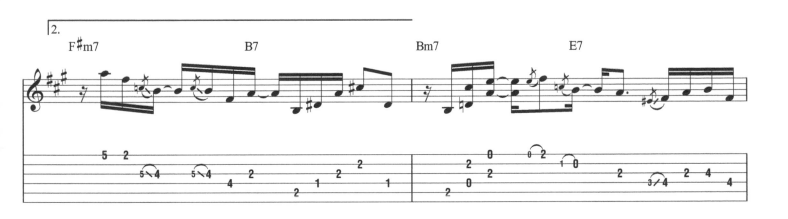

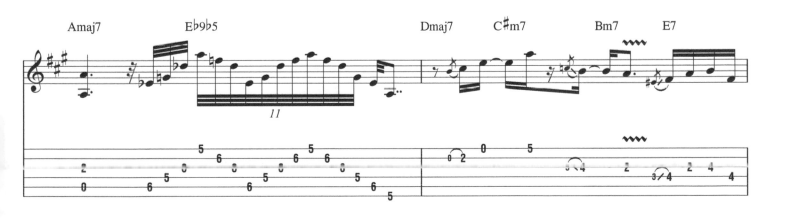

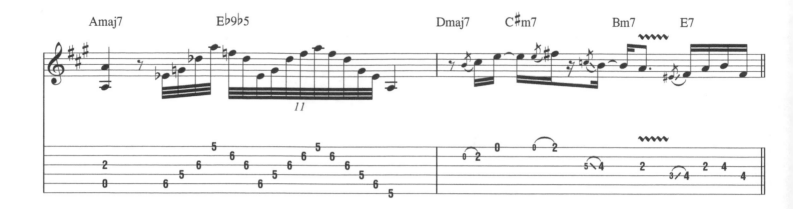

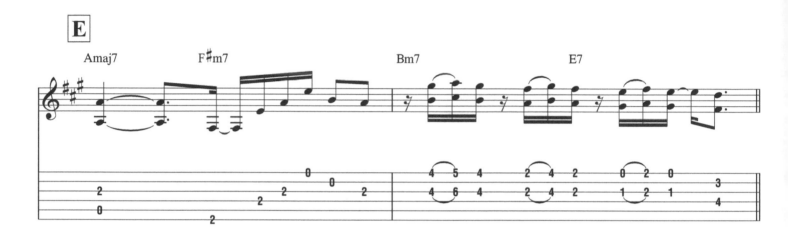

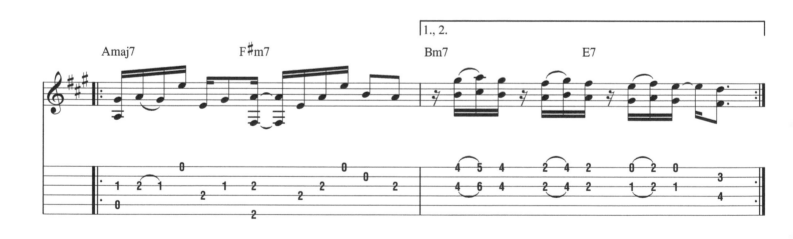

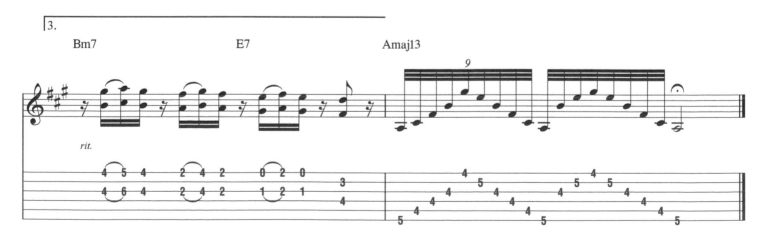